UKULELE
TOP HITS OF 2022

ISBN 978-1-7051-7633-7

HAL•LEONARD®

Visit Hal Leonard Online at
www.halleonard.com

World headquarters, contact:
Hal Leonard
7777 West Bluemound Road
Milwaukee, WI 53213
Email: info@halleonard.com

In Europe, contact:
Hal Leonard Europe Limited
1 Red Place
London, W1K 6PL
Email: info@halleonardeurope.com

In Australia, contact:
Hal Leonard Australia Pty. Ltd.
4 Lentara Court
Cheltenham, Victoria, 3192 Australia
Email: info@halleonard.com.au

As It Was

Words and Music by Harry Styles, Thomas Hull and Tyler Johnson

1. Hold-ing me back, __ grav-i-ty's hold-ing me back.
2. An-swer the phone, _ "Har-ry, you're no good a-lone. _

I want you to hold out the palm of your hand. Why don't we
Why are you sit-ting at home on the floor? What kind of

leave it at that? __ Noth-ing to say __
pills are you on?" __ Ring-ing the bell __

when ev-'ry-thing gets in the way. __ Seems you can-
and no-bod-y's com-ing to help. __ Your dad-dy

_____ it's not the same as _____ it was,

as _____ it was, as _____ it

was. _____ You know _____ it's not the

1. 2. **Bridge**

same. same. Go home, get a - head,

light - speed in - ter - net. I don't want to talk a - bout the way that it was. _____

Leave A - mer - i - ca, two kids fol - low her. I don't want to talk a - bout who's

do - ing it first. ___ *(Instrumental)*

Outro-Chorus

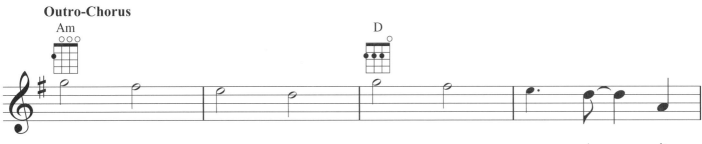

As ___ it

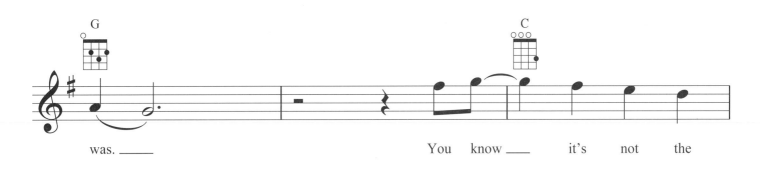

was. ___ You know ___ it's not the

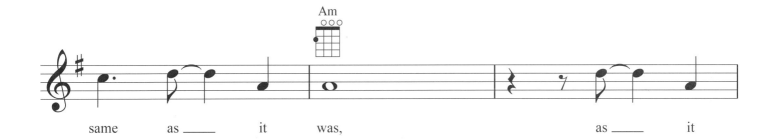

same as ___ it was, as ___ it

was, as ___ it was. ___

(Instrumental)

Bam Bam

Words and Music by Camila Cabello, Ed Sheeran, Scott Harris, Eric Frederic, Edgar Barrera and Cheche Alara

First note

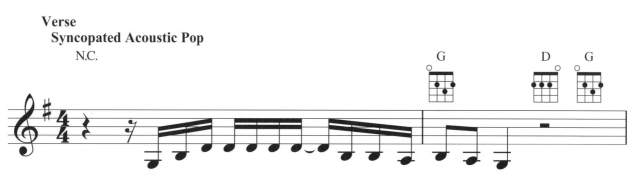

Verse
Syncopated Acoustic Pop

Female: 1. You said you hat-ed the o - cean, but you're surf-ing now.

I said I'd love you for life, __ but I just sold our house.

We were kids at the start, _ I guess we're grown-ups now, __ mm.

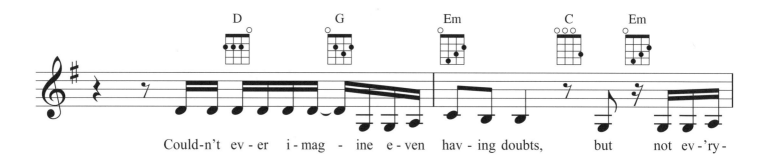

Could-n't ev - er i - mag - ine e - ven hav - ing doubts, but not ev - 'ry-

Interlude

me. Ba da bam bam bam bam _____ bam bam. Ba da bam bam bam bam _

_____ bam bam. Ba da bam bam bam bam _____ bam bam. Ba da bam bam bam bam.

Ba da bam bam bam bam _____ bam bam. Ba da bam bam bam bam _

To Coda

_____ bam bam. Ba da bam bam bam bam _____ bam bam. Ba da bam bam bam bam.

Verse

Male: 2. It's been a hell of a year, _ thank God we made it out.

Yeah, we were rid-ing a wave _ and try-ing not to drown. And on the

surface I held it together, but underneath __ I sorta came around. Where would I

be? You're all that I need. __ My world, __ baby, you hold me down. You always

D.S. al Coda

hold me down, _____ but

Coda

Póngan-ie a-zú-car mi gen-te!

Bridge

Y si-gue bai-lan-do. *Y si-gue bai-lan-do.*

Y si-gue bai-lan-do. *Y si-gue bai-lan-do.*
(Keep danc - ing, yeah. Keep danc - ing, yeah.)

9

Y si - gue bai - lan - do. _____   Y si - gue bai - lan - do.

Y si - gue bai - lan - do. _____

A - sí es la vi - da, _

Chorus

_____ sí.   Yeah, that's just life, ba - by.   Yeah, love came a - round _

_____ and it knocked me down, _ but I'm back on my feet.   A - sí es la vi - da, _

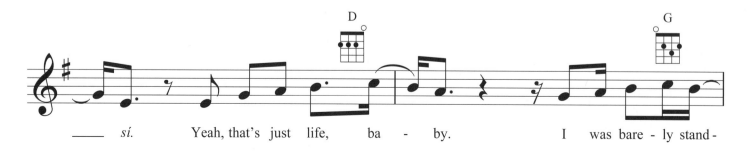

_____ sí.   Yeah, that's just life, ba - by.   I was bare - ly stand -

- ing, but now I'm danc - ing, he's all o - ver me. Now I, now I'm danc - ing. —

Outro

____ (Keep danc - ing, yeah.) Now I, now I'm danc - ing. ____ Now I, now I'm danc - ing. —
Keep danc - ing, yeah.)

Keep danc - ing, yeah.

And now I'm danc - ing. ____ Now I'm danc - ing. ____
Keep danc - ing, yeah. Keep danc - ing, yeah, —

____ yeah, yeah, ____ yeah. ____ Bam bam bam bam.

Carolina

from WHERE THE CRAWDADS SING

Words and Music by Taylor Swift

* *Vocal written one octave higher than sung.*

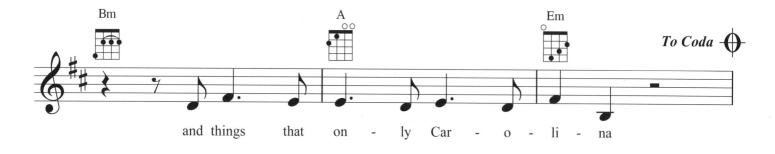

and things that on - ly Car - o - li - na

Interlude

will ev - er know. *(Instrumental)*

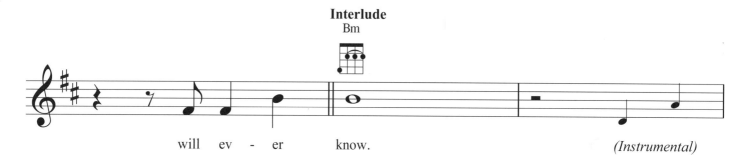

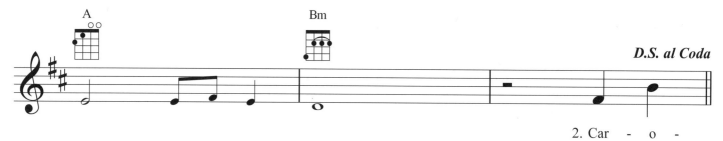

2. Car - o -

Bridge

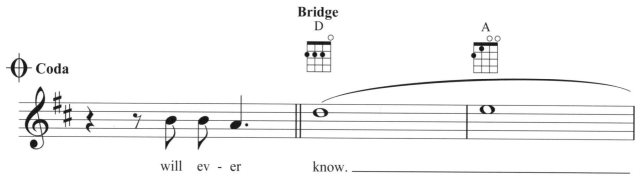

will ev - er know. _____

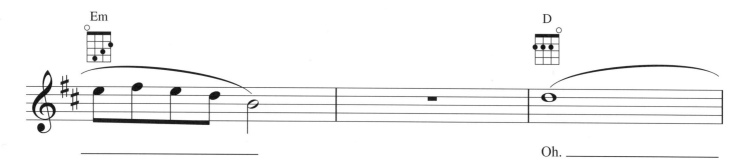

_____ Oh. _____

Oh. _____

Oh. _____

Pre-Chorus

And you did-n't see me here.

here. They nev-er did see me here. _____ No,

you did-n't see me here. They nev-er saw

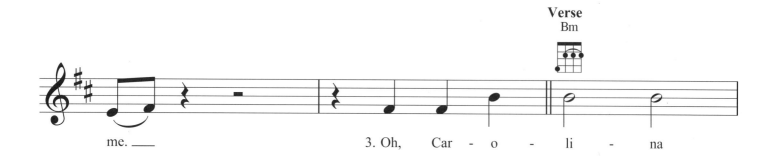

me. ____ 3. Oh, Car - o - li - na

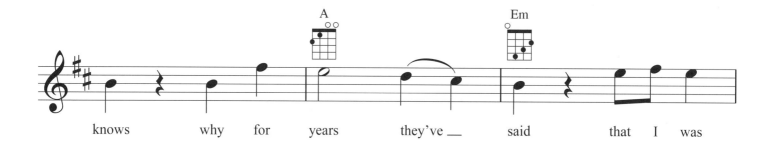

knows why for years they've ___ said that I was

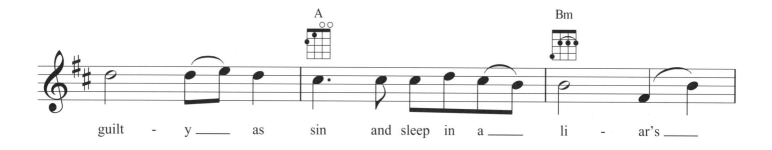

guilt - y ___ as sin and sleep in a ___ li - ar's ___

bed. But the sleep comes fast and I'll

meet no ___ ghosts. It's bet - ween me, the sand and the

sea, Car - o - li - na ___ knows.

Light Switch

Words and Music by Charlie Puth, Jacob Kasher Hindlin and Jacob Torrey

don't wan - na fight this (no). You know how to just

make me want... You turn me on like a light switch

when you're mov - ing your bod - y a - round ___ and a - round. ___

_____ You've got ___ me in a tight grip.

1.

You know how to just make me want you, ba - by.

2., 3.

Bridge

you, ba - by. _____ Come on, ___ come on, come on, come

on, come on ___ and show me how you do. _____ You want, _

___ you want, you want, you want, you wan - na keep me want - ing you. _

Come on, ___ come on, come on, come on, come on ___ and show

me how you do. _____ You want, ___ you want, you want, you

want, you wan - na keep me want - ing you. _
You turn me

Chorus

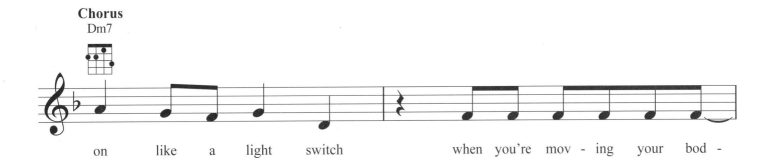

on   like   a   light   switch   when   you're   mov - ing   your   bod -

- y   a - round ___   and   a - round. _____   Now   I ___

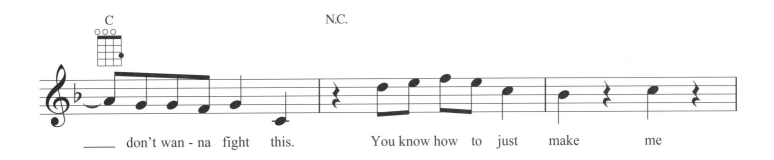

___   don't   wan - na   fight   this.   You   know   how   to   just   make   me

D.S. al Coda
(take 2nd ending)

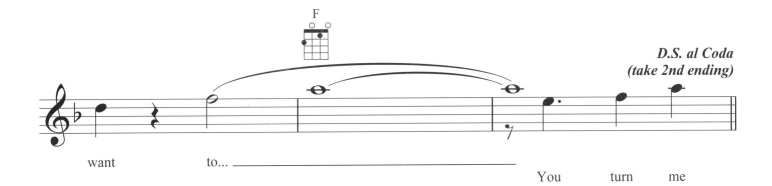

want   to... _____   You   turn   me

Coda

me   want - ing   you. _____

Enemy

Words and Music by Daniel Coulter Reynolds, Daniel Wayne Sermon, Benjamin Arthur McKee, Daniel James Platzman, Justin Tranter, Mattias Larsson and Robin Fredriksson

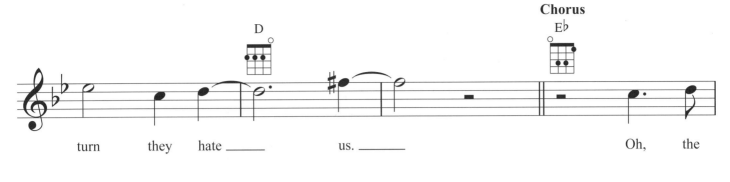

turn they hate _____ us. _____   Oh, the

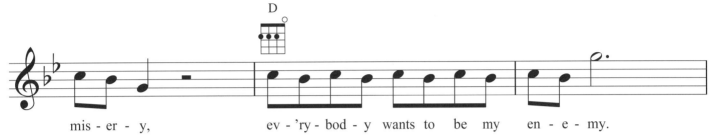

mis - er - y,   ev - 'ry - bod - y wants to be my en - e - my.

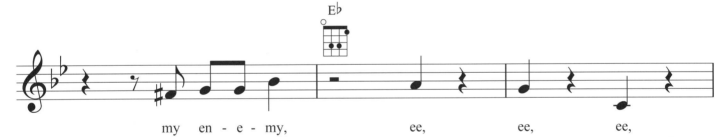

Spare   the   sym - pa - thy,   ev - 'ry - bod - y wants to be

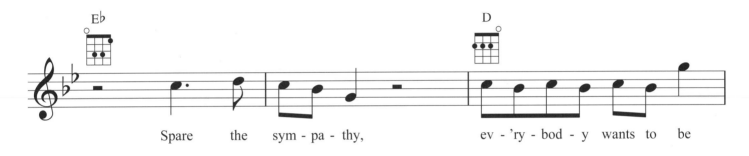

my en - e - my,   ee,   ee,   ee,

ee.
(Look out ___ for your-self!)   My en - e - my,   ee,   (Look,   look,

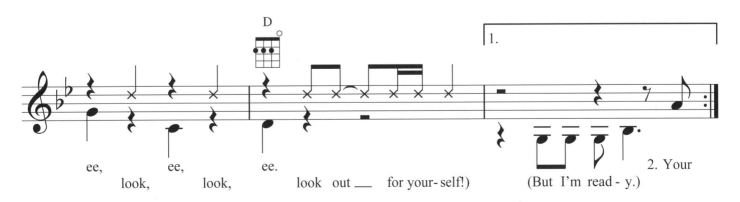

ee,   ee,   ee.   look out ___ for your-self!)
look,   look,   look out ___ for your-self!)   (But I'm read - y.)   2. Your

23

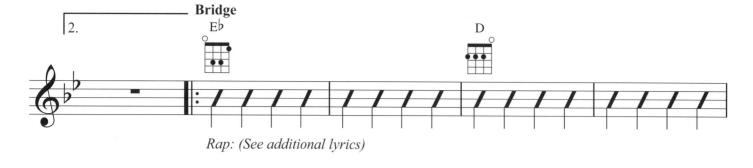

Rap: (See additional lyrics)

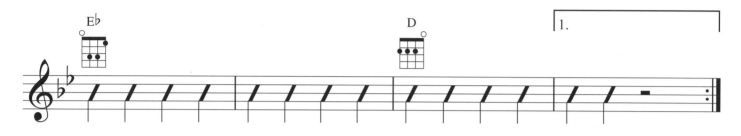

Ev - 'ry - bod - y wants to be my

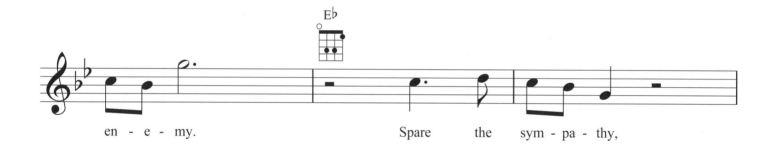

en - e - my.   Spare   the   sym - pa - thy,

ev - 'ry - bod - y wants to be   my en - e - my.   Oh,   the

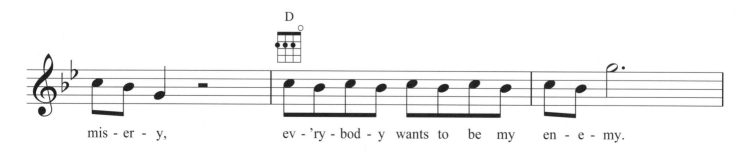

mis - er - y,   ev - 'ry - bod - y wants to be my en - e - my.

Spare the sym - pa - thy, ev - 'ry - bod - y wants to be

Outro

my en - e - my. Pray a - way, I swear, I'll nev - er be a

saint, no way, my en - e - my. Pray a - way, I

swear, I'll nev - er be a saint. (Look out _____ for your- self!)

Additional Lyrics

Rap: Uh, look, okay
I'm hopin' that somebody pray for me
I'm prayin' that somebody hope for me
I'm stayin' where nobody 'posed to be
P-p-posted
Being a wreck of emotions
Ready to go whenever, just let me know
The road is long, so put the pedal into the floor
The enemy on my trail, my energy unavailable
I'm-a tell 'em, "Hasta luego"
They wanna plot on my trot to the top
I been outta shape thinkin' out the box, I'm an astronaut
I blasted off the planet rock to cause catastrophe
And it matters more because I had it not
Had I thought about wreaking havoc
On an opposition, kinda shockin' they wanted static
With precision, I'm automatic quarterback
I ain't talkin' sackin', pack it
Pack it up, I don't panic, batter-batter up
Who the baddest? It don't matter 'cause we at your throat

Freedom

Words and Music by Tierce Person, Autumn Rowe, Andrae Alexander and Jonathan Batiste

- guage. The way that you walk, you can't ___ con - tain ___

___ it.   Is it the shoes? ___ Jumped up, kan - ga - roo. ___

___ We're o - ver - due ___ for a lit - tle more pranc -

- ing.   Now is your time, ___ (it's your right) you can shine ___

___ (it's al - right). ___ If you do, ___ I'm - a do, too. ___

Chorus

___ When I move my bod - y just like this,

I don't know why, but I feel like free - dom. —

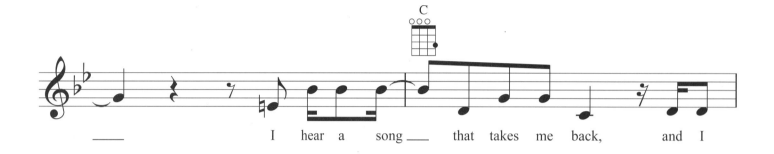

— I hear a song — that takes me back, and I

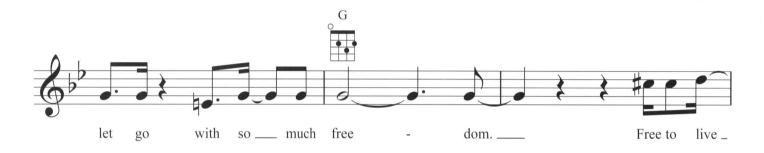

let go with so — much free - dom. — Free to live —

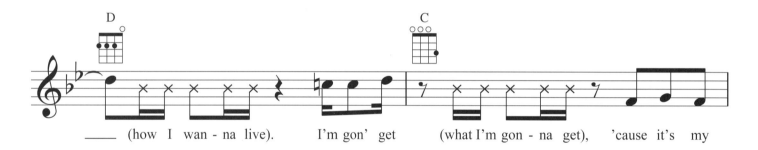

— (how I wan - na live). I'm gon' get (what I'm gon - na get), 'cause it's my

free - dom. — 2. The rea - son we get down — is to get back up. —

If some - one's a - round, — go on, — let them look. —

You can't stand still, _____ this ain't no drill. _

More than cheap thrills. _ Now is your time, _

_____ (it's your right) you can shine _____ (it's al - right). _ If you do, _

_____ I'm - a do, too. _____

Bridge 1

'Cause when I look up to the stars,

I know ex - act - ly who we are, 'cause then I

29

Vocal written one octave higher than sung.

give you the whole shake. I'm stuck to the

Let me see _____ you wob -

G

dance floor with the, with the whole tape, with the,

ble.

D7

with the, with the whole tape. I say yeah _____ (yeah), _ oh yeah _

Can you make _ it break?

C7   G

_____ (oh yeah). 'Cause you do, I'm - a do, too.

Let me see _ you wob - ble.

Vocal written at recorded pitch.

Glimpse of Us

Words and Music by Joji Kusunoki, Connor McDonough, Riley McDonough, Joel Castillo and Alexis Kesselman

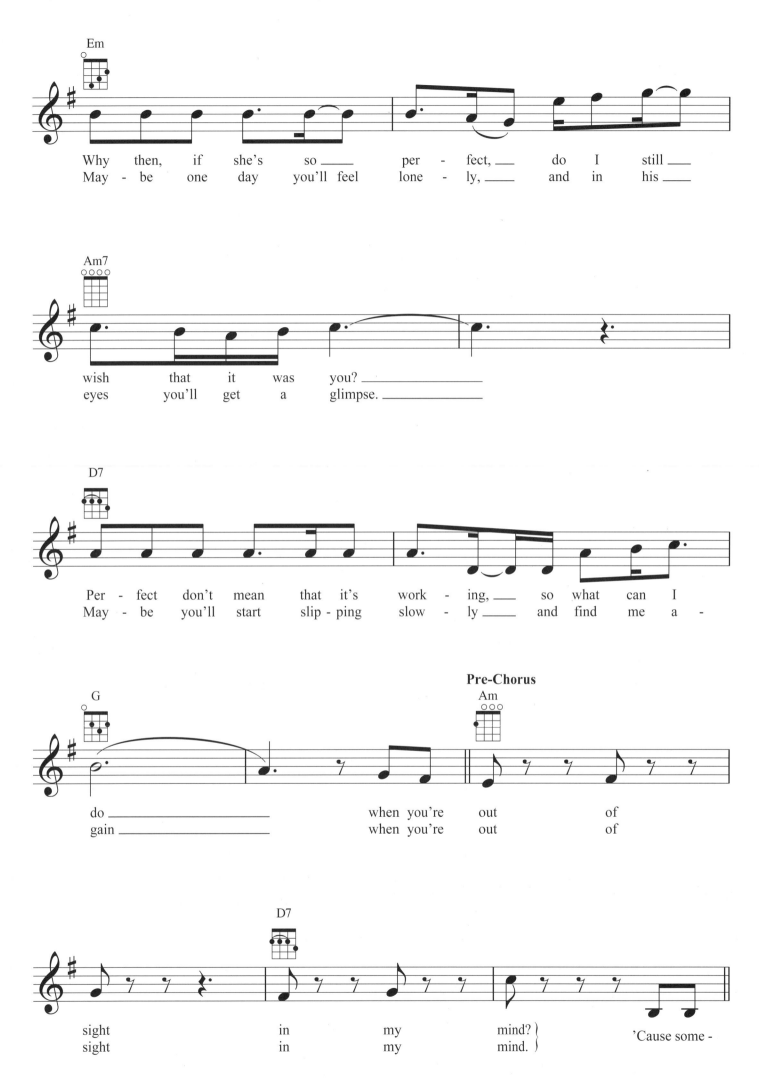

times I look in her eyes, and that's where I

find a glimpse of us. _____ And I

try to fall for her touch, ___ but I'm think - ing

of the way it was. _____ Said I'm ___

fine, and said I moved _ on. I'm on - ly

To Coda

here pass - ing time in her ___ arms, hop - ing I'll find a

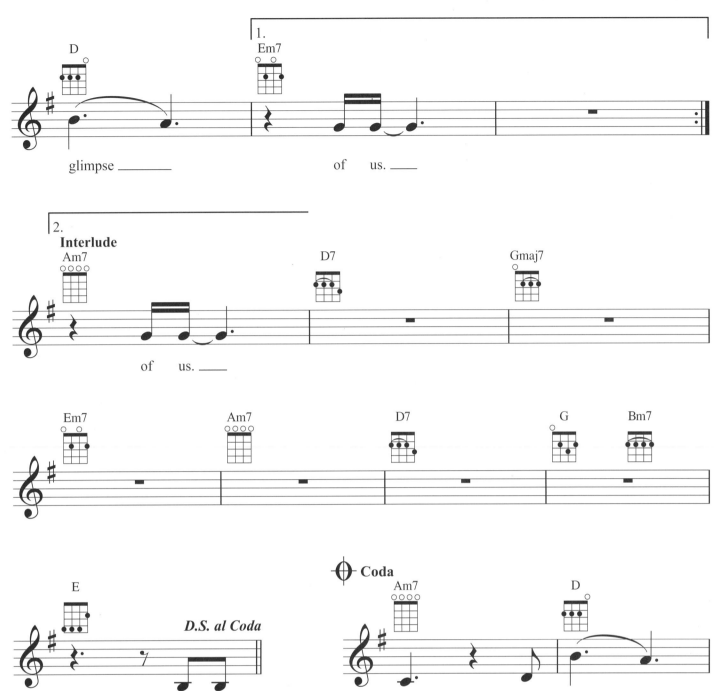

glimpse _____ of us. ____

Interlude

of us. ____

D.S. al Coda

'Cause some -

 **Coda**

find   a   glimpse ____

Outro

of us. ____

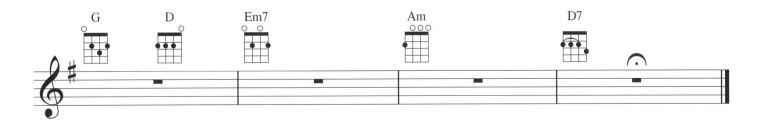

Hold My Hand

from TOP GUN: MAVERICK
Words and Music by Stefani Germanotta and Michael Tucker

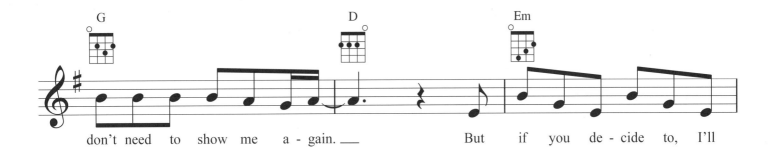

don't need to show me a - gain. ___ But if you de - cide to, I'll

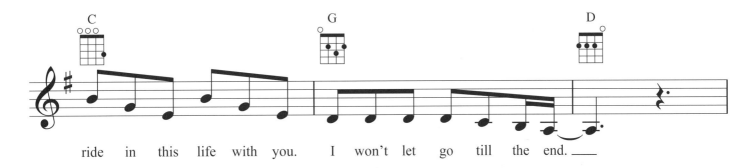

ride in this life with you. I won't let go till the end. ___

Chorus

N.C.

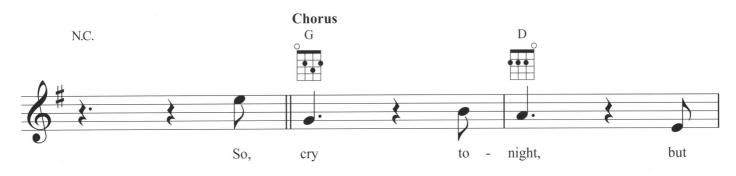

So, cry to - night, but

don't you let go of my hand. ___ You can cry ___ ev - 'ry last ___

___ tear, I won't leave till I un - der - stand. ___

1.   2.

Prom - ise { me, / you'll } just hold my hand. ___ 2. Raise your hand. ___ Hold my

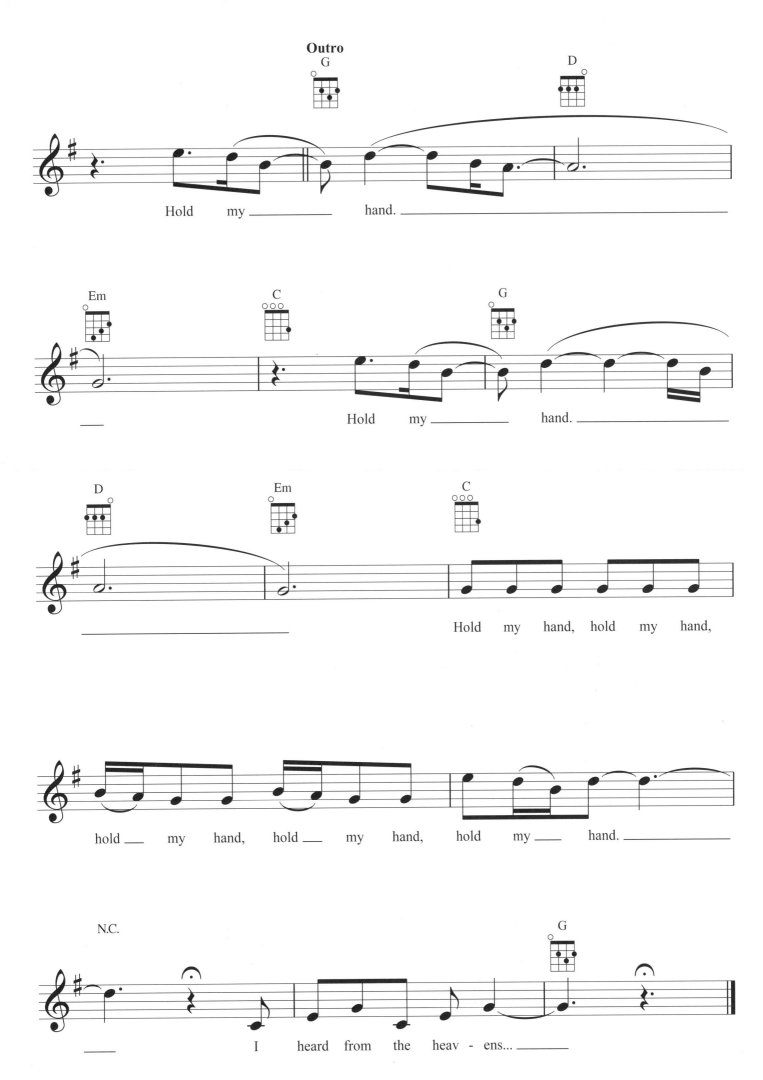

In the Stars

Words and Music by Benson Boone, Michael Pollack and Jason Evigan

bur - ied my faith ___ with you. ___ I'm

scream-ing at a God ___ I don't know if I ___ be-lieve in, 'cause

I don't know what else I can do. ___ I'm still

℅ Chorus

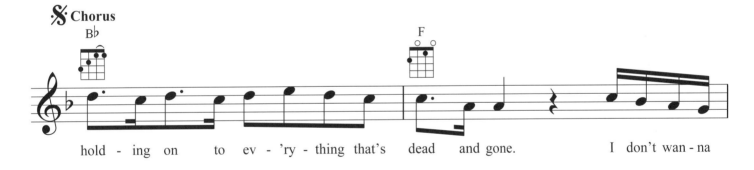

hold - ing on to ev - 'ry - thing that's dead and gone. I don't wan - na

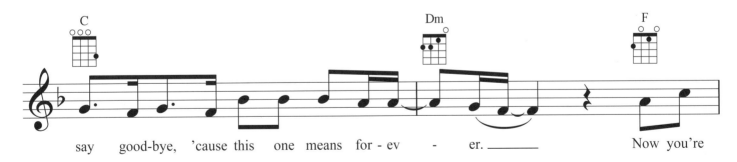

say good-bye, 'cause this one means for - ev - er. ___ Now you're

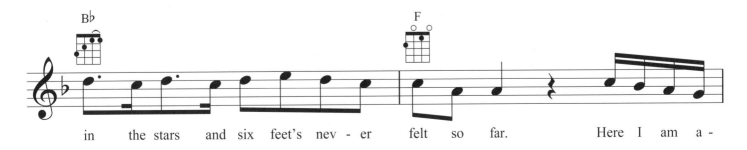

in the stars and six feet's nev - er felt so far. Here I am a-

lone be-tween the heav-ens and ___ the em - bers. _____ Oh, _____ it

hurts so hard _____ for a mil - lion dif-f'rent rea - sons. You took the

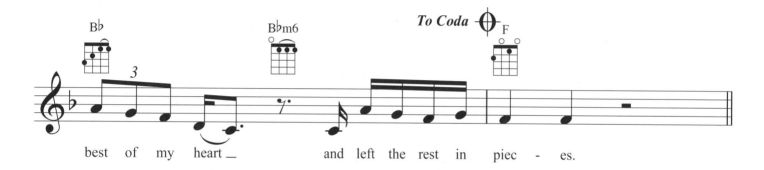

best of my heart ___ and left the rest in piec - es.

Verse

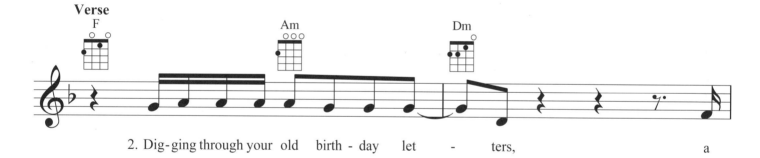

2. Dig-ging through your old birth-day let - ters, a

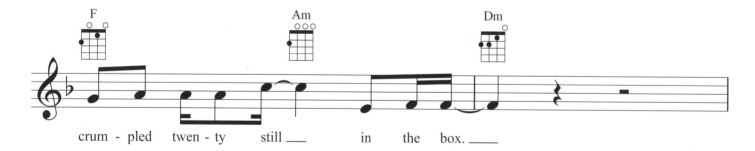

crum - pled twen - ty still ___ in the box. ___

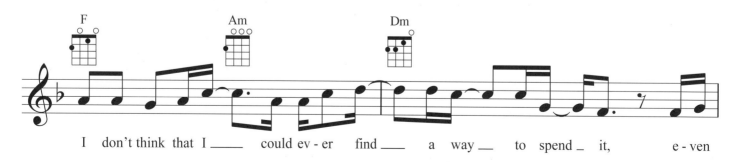

I don't think that I _____ could ev - er find ___ a way __ to spend __ it, e - ven

44

dead and gone. I don't wan-na say good-bye, 'cause this one means for-

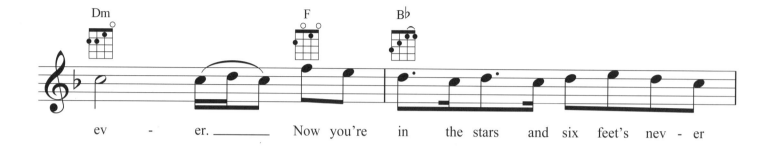

ev - er. _____ Now you're in the stars and six feet's nev - er

felt so far. Here I am a - lone be-tween the heav - ens and __ the em -

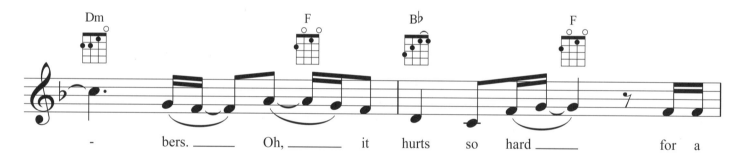

- bers. ____ Oh, _____ it hurts so hard _____ for a

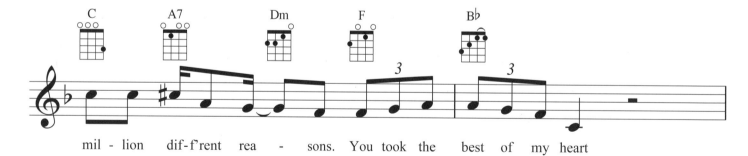

mil - lion dif-f'rent rea - sons. You took the best of my heart

and left the rest in piec - es.

Nobody Like U

from TURNING RED

Music and Lyrics by Billie Eilish and Finneas O'Connell

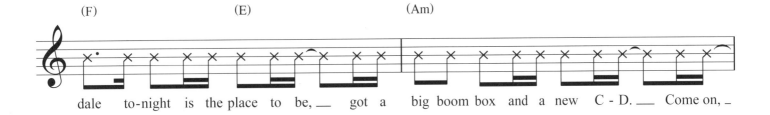

(F)   (E)   (Am)

dale to-night is the place to be, __ got a   big boom box and a new C - D. __ Come on, __

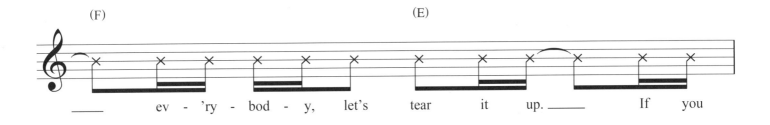

(F)   (E)

__ ev - 'ry - bod - y, let's tear it up. _____ If you

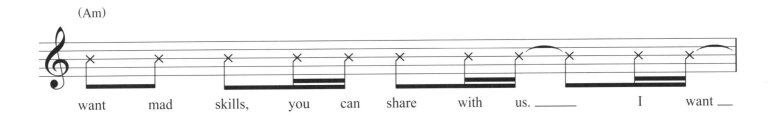

(Am)

want mad skills, you can share with us. _____ I want __

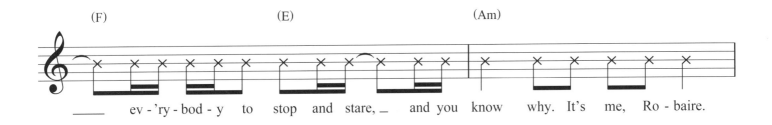

(F)   (E)   (Am)

__ ev - 'ry - bod - y to stop and stare, _ and you know why. It's me, Ro - baire.

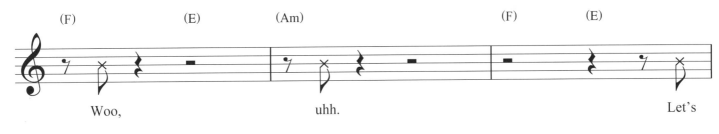

(F)   (E)   (Am)   (F)   (E)

Woo,   uhh.   Let's

(Am)

D.S. al Coda

go.   You're nev - er not on my

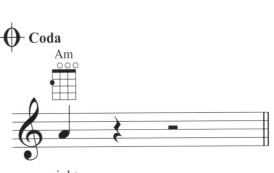

Coda

Am

right.

Interlude

Li, li, li, li, li, like you.   Li, li, li, li, li, like you.

Li, li, li, li, li, like you.   Like _ you, like _ you.

Li, li, li, li, li, like you.   Li, li, li, li, li, like you.

Li, li, li, li, __ like _ you.   Like _ you. 2. I've nev - er met no -

Verse

bod - y ____ like __ you. __ Had friends and I've had

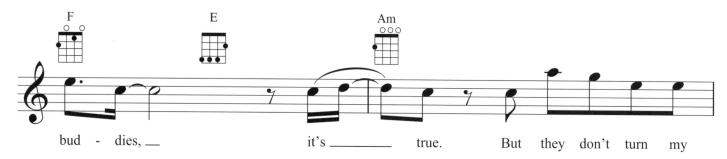

bud - dies, __ it's _____ true. But they don't turn my

tum - my _____ the way ___ you ___ do. I've nev - er met no -

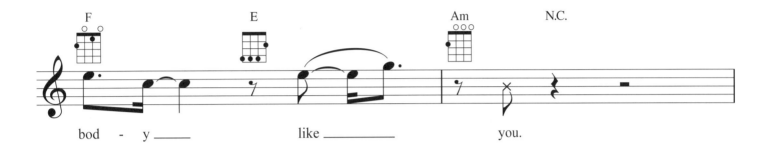

bod - y _____ like _____ you.

Chorus

You're nev - er not on my mind, oh my, oh

my. I'm nev - er not by your side, your side, your

side. I'm nev - er gon - na let you cry, oh cry, don't

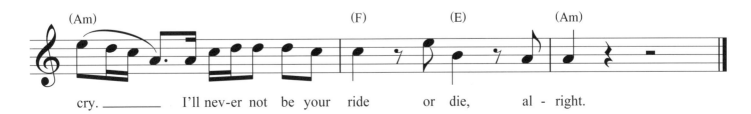

cry. _____ I'll nev-er not be your ride or die, al - right.

Love Me More

Words and Music by Sam Smith, Tor Hermansen, James Napier and Mikkel Eriksen

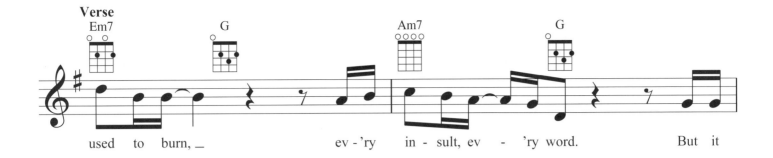

used to burn, ___ ev-'ry in - sult, ev - 'ry word. But it

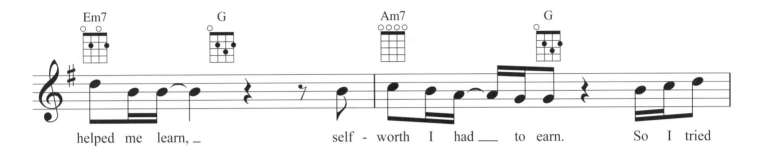

helped me learn, ___ self - worth I had ___ to earn. So I tried

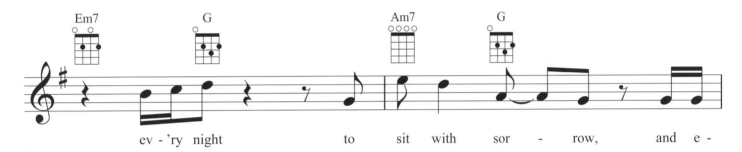

ev - 'ry night to sit with sor - row, and e -

D.C. al Coda

ven - tual - ly ___ it set me free. ___

Coda

love me more, just a lit - tle bit.

Bridge

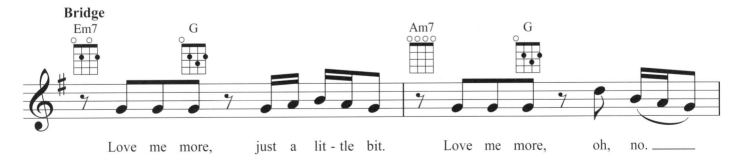

Love me more, just a lit - tle bit. Love me more, oh, no. ___

Love me more, just a lit-tle bit. Love me more. 2. I

Verse

used to cry _____ my-self to sleep _ at night. I'd

blame the sky _____ when the mess was in _ my mind. I could-n't see,

I could-n't breathe, so I sat with sor - row, and e-

ven-tual-ly _____ it set me free. _____

Chorus

Have you ev-er felt like be-ing some-bod-y else, _____

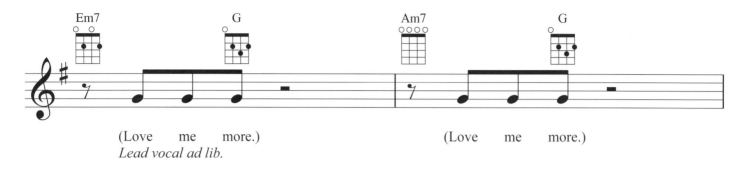

(Love   me   more.)   (Love   me   more.)
Lead vocal ad lib.

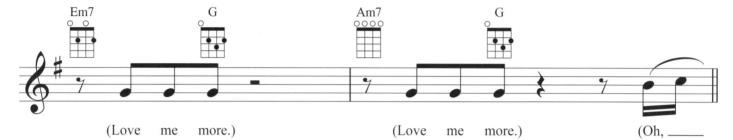

(Love   me   more.)   (Love   me   more.)   (Oh, ____

Outro

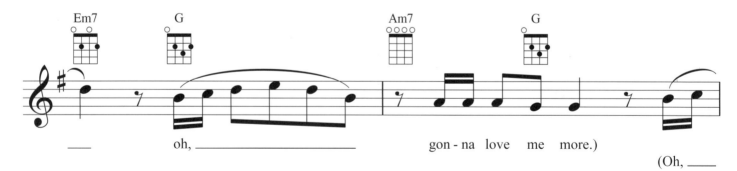

____   oh, _____   gon - na love me more.)   (Oh, ____

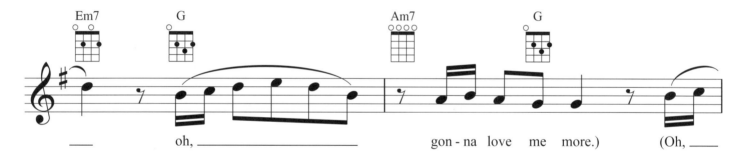

____   oh, _____   gon - na love me more.)   (Oh, ____

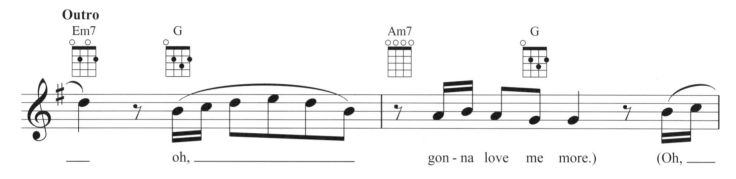

____   oh, _____   gon - na love me more.)
                                                                                (Oh, ____

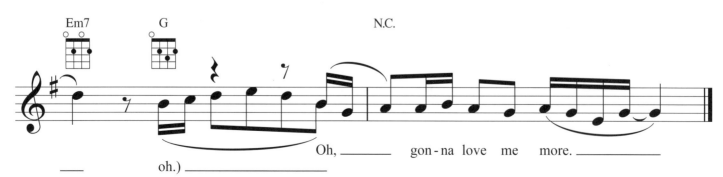

                                    Oh, ____   gon - na love me more. _____
____   oh.) _____

Numb Little Bug

Words and Music by Emily Beihold, Nicholas Lopez and Andrew DeCaro

same   as _____ me.   Do   you   ev - er   get   a

𝄇 Pre-Chorus 2

F   G   Am7

lit - tle   bit   tired   of   life? ___   Like   you're   not ___ real - ly

F   G   Am7

hap - py   but   you   don't   wan - na   die? ___   Like   you're   hang - in'   by   a

F   Em   Am

thread __   but   you   got - ta   sur - vive, _____   'cause   you   got - ta   sur - vive? __

E7

___   Like   your   bod - y's   in   the

F   G   Am7

room __   but   you're   not   real - ly   there? __   Like   you   have   em - pa - thy   in -

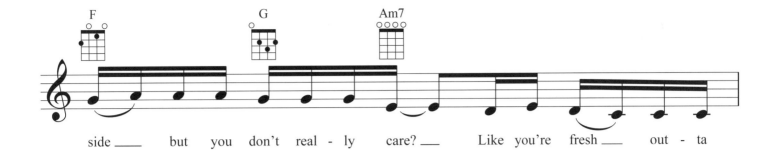

side ___ but you don't real - ly care? ___ Like you're fresh ___ out - ta

love ___ but it's been in the air? _____ Am I past ___ re - pair? _

Chorus

___ A lit - tle bit tired ___ of tryin' to care when I

don't. A lit - tle bit tired ___ of quick re - pairs to

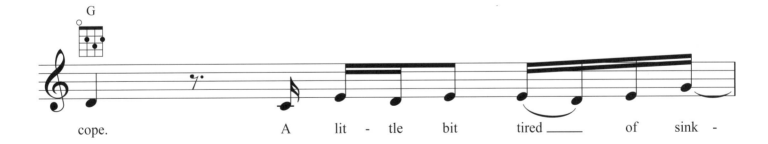

cope. A lit - tle bit tired _____ of sink -

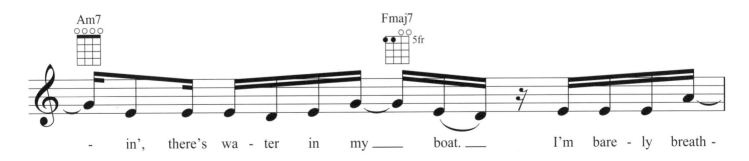

- in', there's wa - ter in my ___ boat. ___ I'm bare - ly breath -

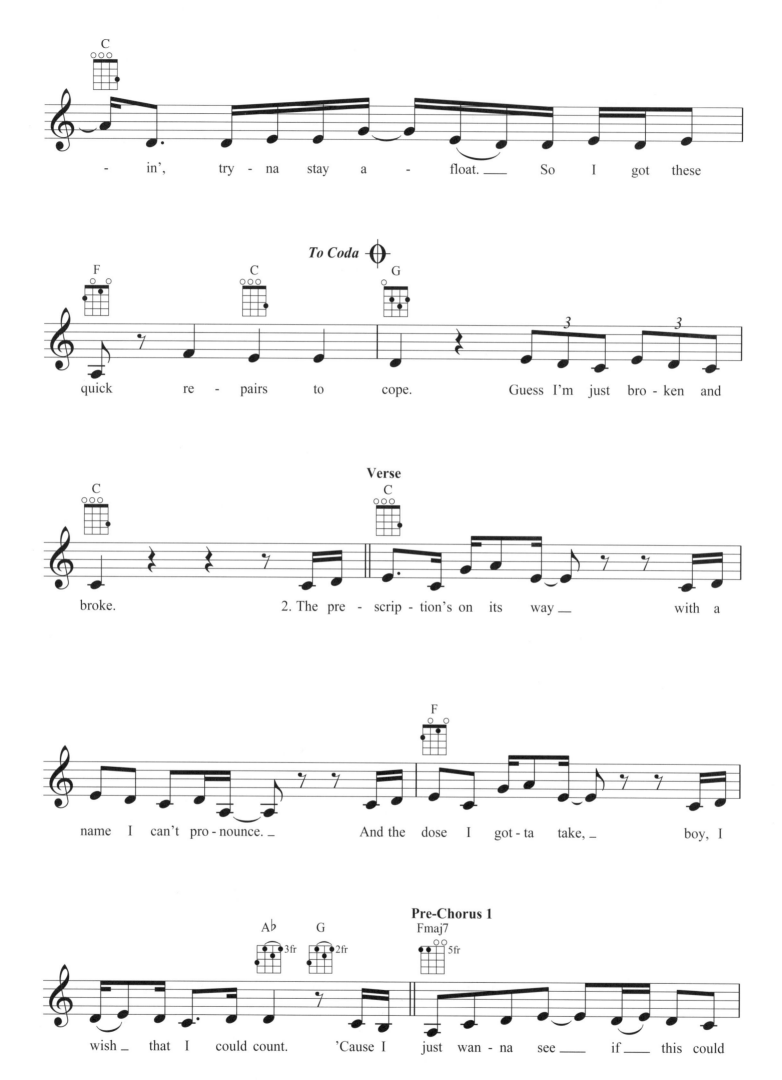

- in', try - na stay a - float. ___ So I got these

quick re - pairs to cope. Guess I'm just bro - ken and

broke. 2. The pre - scrip - tion's on its way ___ with a

name I can't pro - nounce. _ And the dose I got - ta take, _ boy, I

wish _ that I could count. 'Cause I just wan - na see ___ if ___ this could

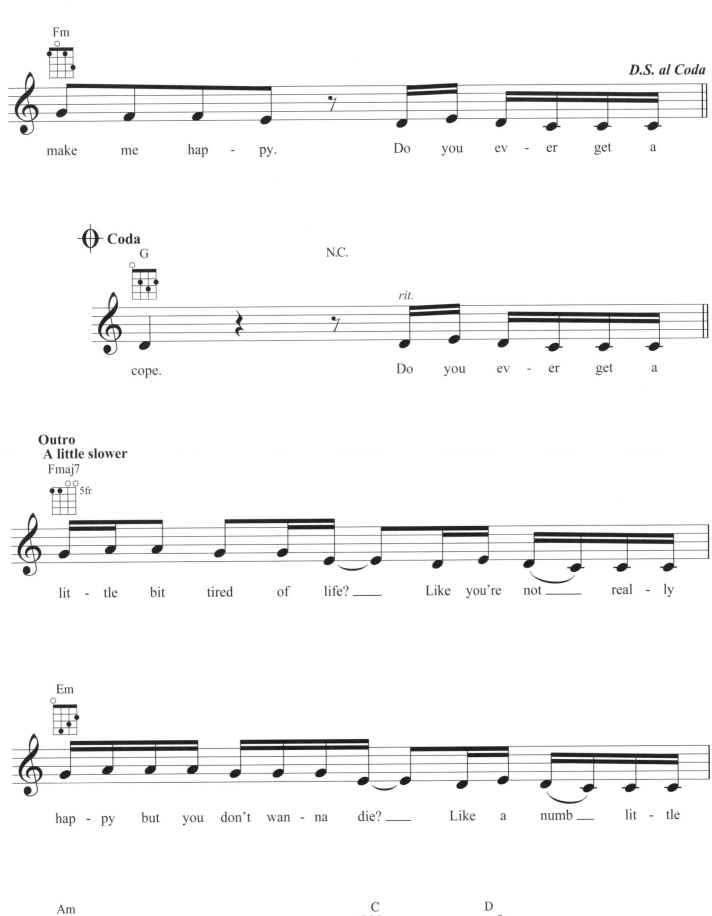

Fm

D.S. al Coda

make me hap - py. Do you ev - er get a

⊕ Coda

G N.C. *rit.*

cope. Do you ev - er get a

Outro
A little slower

Fmaj7 5fr

lit - tle bit tired of life? ____ Like you're not ____ real - ly

Em

hap - py but you don't wan - na die? ____ Like a numb ____ lit - tle

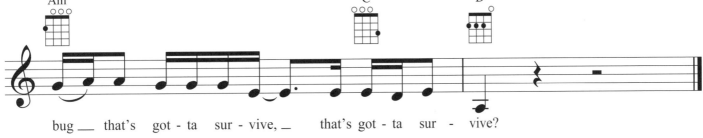

Am **C** **D**

bug ___ that's got - ta sur - vive, ___ that's got - ta sur - vive?

On My Way

from MARRY ME
Words and Music by Leroy James Clampitt, Ivy Adara and Michael Pollack

Bm · A · G

I was nev-er lost, _____ I was just pass-ing through. I was on my way to you. _

Verse

D · D

_____ 2. Hope was hope-less, faith was run-ning.

G

Did-n't no-tice you were com-ing through. You were on your way, too.

D

And you don't be-lieve in "meant to be," but

G

some-how you were meant for me, it's true. Yeah, you were on your way, _ too. _

Chorus

D · Bm · A

_____ Ev-'ry heart-break was a yel-low brick road

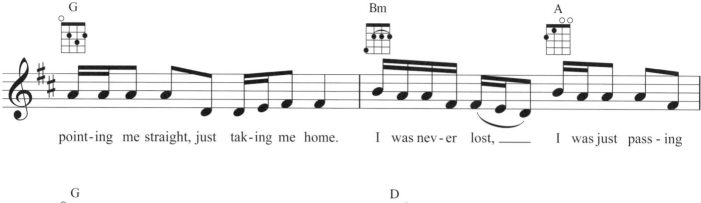

point-ing me straight, just tak-ing me home. I was nev-er lost, _____ I was just pass-ing

through. I was on my way to you. _____ I was on my way to you. _

_ I was on my way to you. _____ I was on my way to you. _____

Bridge

_____ Oh, _____ I'm on _____ my way, _ on _ my way _ to you. On _

_____ my way, _ on _ my way _ to you. On _____ my way, _ on _ my way _ to you. _____

_____ Oh, _____ I'm on _____ my way, _ I'm on _____ my way. _ (On _

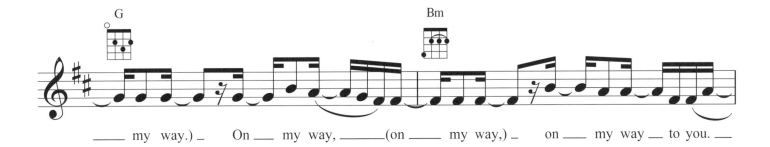

____ my way.) _ On __ my way, _____(on ____ my way,) _ on ___ my way _ to you. ___

Chorus

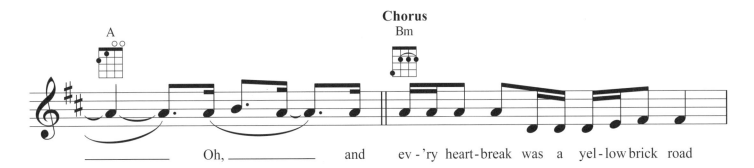

_____ Oh, _____ and ev-'ry heart-break was a yel-low brick road

point-ing me straight, just tak-ing me home. I was nev-er lost, ____ I was just pass - ing ___

Outro

___ through _ on __ my way _ to you. Ooh, _____ ooh. _____

_____ On __ my way _ to you. _____ Oh, __ my dar - ling, I'm on _

N.C.(D)

rit.

___ my way. _ _(Instrumental)_

'Til You Can't

Words and Music by Ben Stennis and Matt Rogers

'til you can't.
'til you can't.

2. You can

If you got a chance, __

Chorus

_____ take __ it, take __ it while you got __ a chance. __

__ If you got a dream, _____ chase __ it 'cause a dream __

__ won't chase you back. __ If you're gon - na love __ some - bod - y, hold __

___ them as long __ and as strong __ and as close __ as you can _

___ 'til you can't.

Verse

3. There's a box of greas - y parts _

___ sit - ting in the trunk __ of that six - ty - five, ___ still

wait - ing on you and your __ gran - dad __ to bring it back _ to life. _

___ You can al - ways get a - round __ to fix - ing up _

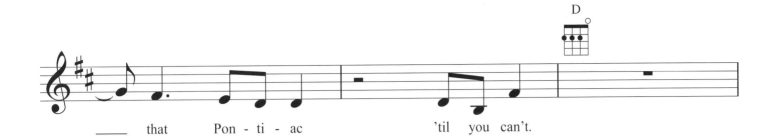

_____ that Pon - ti - ac   'til you can't.

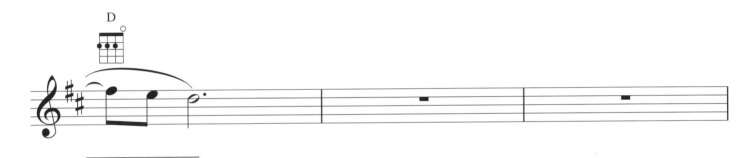

D.S. al Coda

If you got a chance, _____

Coda

_____ 'til you can't. _____

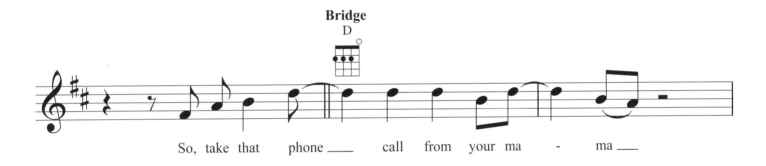

Bridge

So, take that phone _____ call from your ma - ma _____

and just talk a - way. _____ 'Cause you'll nev - er know _____

_____ how bad _____ you'll wan - na _____ 'til you can't _____ some -

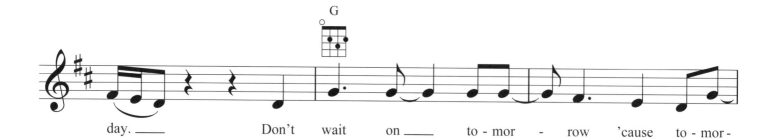

day. ____ Don't wait on ____ to-mor-row 'cause to-mor-

- row may not show. ___ Say your sor-rys, your I love ___

____ yous, 'cause man, you nev-er know. _ If you got a chance, _

Chorus

_____ take ___ it, take ___ it while you got ___ a chance.

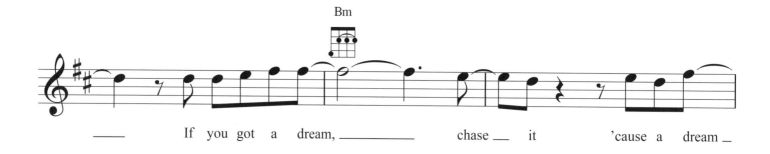

___ If you got a dream, _____ chase ___ it 'cause a dream _

___ won't chase you back. ___ If you're gon-na love _

some - bod - y, hold them as long and as strong

1.

and as close as you can 'til you can't.

2.

Outro

Yeah, if you got a chance, un - til you can't.

'Til you can't.

Yeah.

Take it.

Until I Found You

Words and Music by Emily Beihold and Stephen Sanchez

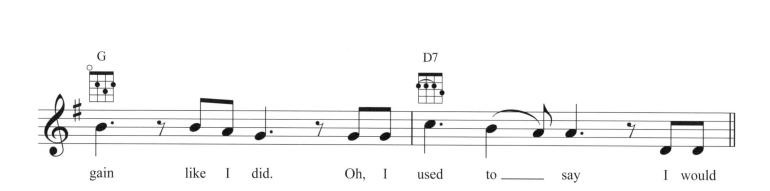

Running Up That Hill

featured in the fourth season of the Netflix series STRANGER THINGS
Words and Music by Kate Bush

And if I on-ly could, _ I'd make a

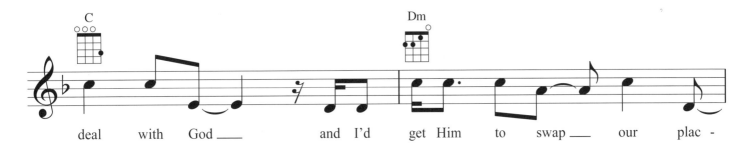

deal with God ___ and I'd get Him to swap ___ our plac -

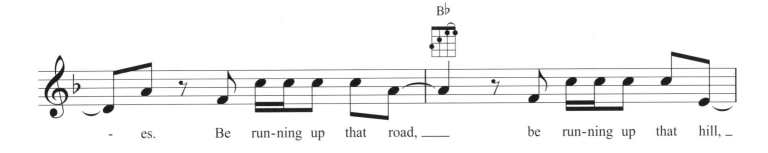

- es. Be run-ning up that road, ___ be run-ning up that hill, _

___ be run - ning up that build - ing.

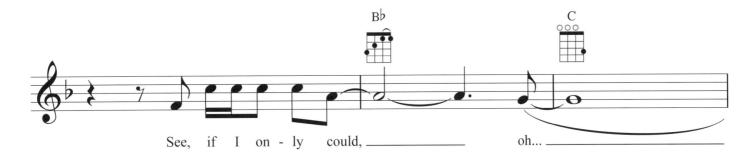

See, if I on - ly could, _____ oh... _____

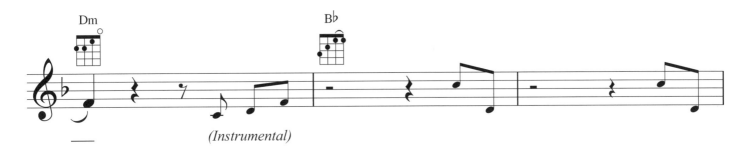

_ *(Instrumental)*

To Coda ⊕ -Verse

2. You don't wan - na hurt __

__ me, but see how deep the bul - let lies. __

__ Un - a - ware I'm tear - ing you a - sun -

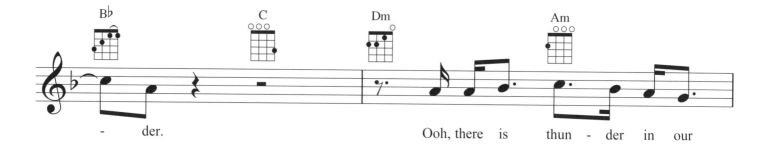

- der. Ooh, there is thun - der in our

hearts. __ Is there so much hate for the ones we love? _

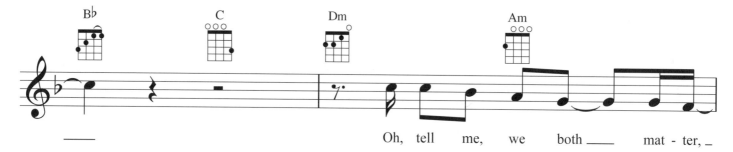

__ Oh, tell me, we both __ mat - ter, _

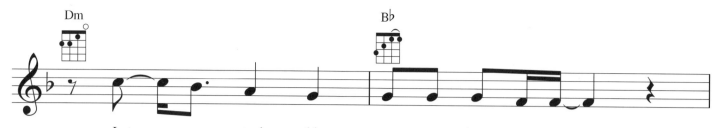

Let ___ me steal this mo - ment from you now. ___

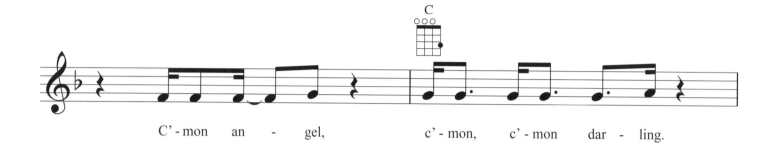

C' - mon an - gel, c' - mon, c' - mon dar - ling.

Let's ___ ex - change the ex - pe - ri - ence,

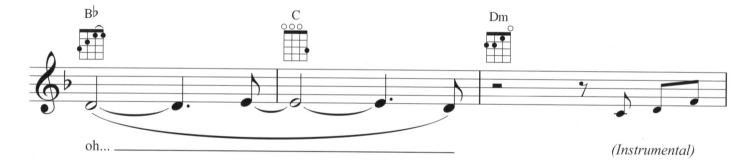

oh... _____ *(Instrumental)*

And if I on - ly could, _

be run - ning up that hill, _____

with no prob - lems. _____

(If I on - ly could, _

_____ I'd be run-ning up that hill. If I on - ly could, _

_____ I'd be run-ning up that hill.) _____